POWERFUL CONFESSIONS FOR VICTORIOUS CHRISTIAN LIVING

Over 300 Verses of Scripture & Confessions

By Funmi Uzoma

Copyright © 2016 by Funmi Uzoma

POWERFUL CONFESSIONS FOR VICTORIOUS CHRISTIAN LIVING
Over 300 Verses of Scripture & Confessions
by Funmi Uzoma

Printed in the United States of America.

ISBN 9781498459938

All rights reserved solely by the author. The author guarantees all contents are original and do not infringe upon the legal rights of any other person or work. No part of this book may be reproduced in any form without the permission of the author. The views expressed in this book are not necessarily those of the publisher.

Unless otherwise indicated, Scripture quotations taken from the Holy Bible, New Living Translation. Copyright ©1996, 2004, 2007 by Tyndale House Foundation. Used by permission of Tyndale House Publishers, Inc.

www.xulonpress.com

Table of contents

Introduction vii

Attributes of God 9
General Confession 12
Christian Growth 23
Faith 30
Deliverance / Warfare 38
Fear 49
Provision 54
Healing 61
Protection 71
Woman of Virtue 75
The Real Man 78
Mercy of God 80
Church Growth 83
Children 87
Teenagers 90

About the Author 99

Introduction

Words are powerful. Jesus told His disciples in Matthew 17:20, "And Jesus said unto them, Because of your unbelief: for verily I say unto you, If ye have faith as a grain of mustard seed, ye shall say unto this mountain, Remove hence to yonder place; and it shall remove; and nothing shall be impossible unto you." Our faith and utterance is linked to our miracle. It is therefore important to say what we believe. Even the smallest faith backed up with confession of God's word, could birth a miracle. For instance, we earned salvation by believing and confessing that Jesus is Lord. The Bible says, "That if thou shalt confess with thy mouth the Lord Jesus, and shalt believe in thine heart that God hath raised him from the dead, thou shalt be saved. [10] For with the heart man believeth unto righteousness; and with the mouth confession is made unto salvation." (Romans 10:9–10 KJV). Confession of God's word will always bring good results. For instance, God said to Jeremiah, "Thou hast well seen, for I will hasten My word to perform it." (Jeremiah 1: 12 KJV). The Lord watches over His Word. In Isaiah 55:11, the Bible also says, "So shall my word be that goeth forth out of my mouth: it shall not return unto me void, but it shall accomplish that which I please, and it shall prosper in the thing whereto I sent it." Furthermore, the word of God is both an offensive and defensive weapon; biblically described as 'the sword of the Spirit' in Ephesians 6:17. The sword of the

Spirit is one of the major weapons needed in spiritual warfare. When put to use in the battles of life, victory is sure.

Powerful Confessions for Victorious Christian Living offers readers choice scriptures from God's Word to help them in several areas of life, from Christian growth to handling fear, divine healing and comprehending the mercy of God. The verses and confessions enable Christians to understand God's plan for them. Satan is always at war with Christians, trying to hinder them from attaining God's ultimate purpose. God's redemption plan is to save man – spirit, soul and body. The redemption of the spirit is at the new birth, when we are born again. The redemption of the soul is through sanctification. The redemption of the body is at resurrection, when the Lord Jesus returns. The Christian plays a major role in the redemption of his or her soul, because there is a constant war that goes on between the Spirit and the flesh Galatians 5: 17. To win this war the Christian needs the effective use of God's word.

By the help of the Holy Spirit I have put this book together as a tool for every Christian Family.

The Chapter titled 'General Confessions' spans across almost every issue of life, and so can be used as a daily confession. The other chapters should be used as the needs arise. Remember, in 1 Peter 5: 8 the Bible tells us, that our enemy the devil, goes about like a roaring lion, seeking whom he may devour. As a result, it is important we stay on the offensive: sober and vigilant so we are not caught in his web of attacks. When you arm yourself with these confessions, you will live a Victorious Christian Life.

Attributes of God

These scriptures reveal the person of God: who He is, His person, and His nature. Let's appreciate Him for His attributes.

O LORD God of Heaven's Armies! Where is there anyone as mighty as you, O LORD? You are entirely faithful. [9] You rule the oceans. You subdue their storm-tossed waves. [10] You crushed the great sea monster. You scattered your enemies with your mighty arm. [11] The heavens are yours, and the earth is yours; everything in the world is yours-you created it all. [12] You created north and south. Mount Tabor and Mount Hermon praise your name. [13] Powerful is your arm! Strong is your hand! Your right hand is lifted high in glorious strength. [14] Righteousness and justice are the foundation of your throne. Unfailing love and truth walk before you as attendants (Psalm 89:8-14). Who is like unto thee, O Lord, among the gods? Who is like thee, glorious in holiness, fearful in praises, doing wonders? (Exodus 15:11 KJV). The strong right arm of the LORD is raised in triumph. The strong right arm of the LORD has done glorious things! (Psalm 118:16). He is wise in heart, and mighty in strength: who hath hardened himself against him, and hath prospered? (Job 9:4 KJV). "How you have helped the powerless! How you have saved the weak! (Job 26:2). Touching the Almighty, we cannot find him out: he is excellent in power, and in judgment, and in plenty of justice: he will not afflict (Job 37:23 KJV).

Thou art good, and doest good; teach me thy statutes. [72] The law of thy mouth is better unto me than thousands of gold and silver (Psalm 119:68, 72 KJV).

But God is so rich in mercy, and he loved us so much, [5] that even though we were dead because of our sins, he gave us life when he raised Christ from the dead. It is only by God's grace that you have been saved! (Ephesians 2:4-5). I know now that the LORD is greater than all other gods, because he rescued his people from the oppression of the proud Egyptians." (Exodus 18:11). Whatever is good and perfect is a gift coming down to us from God our Father, who created all the lights in the heavens. He never changes or casts a shifting shadow (James 1:17). Ah Lord God! behold, thou hast made the heaven and the earth by thy great power and stretched out arm, and there is nothing too hard for thee: [19] Great in counsel, and mighty in work: for thine eyes are open upon all the ways of the sons of men: to give every one according to his ways, and according to the fruit of his doings: [27] Behold, I am the Lord, the God of all flesh: is there any thing too hard for me? (Jeremiah 32:17, 19, 27 KJV). Holy, holy, holy, is the Lord of hosts: the whole earth is full of his glory (Isaiah 6:3 KJV). Holy, holy, holy, Lord God Almighty, which was, and is, and is to come (Revelation 4:8 KJV). With every bone in my body I will praise him: "LORD, who can compare with you? Who else rescues the helpless from the strong? Who else protects the helpless and poor from those who rob them?" (Psalm 35:10). The LORD passed in front of Moses, calling out, "Yahweh! The LORD! The God of compassion and mercy! I am slow to anger and filled with unfailing love and faithfulness (Exodus 34:6). Jesus looked at them intently and said, "Humanly speaking, it is impossible. But with God everything is possible." (Matthew 19:26). Abraham named the place Yahweh-Yireh (which means "the LORD will provide"). To this day, people still use that name as a proverb: "On the mountain of the LORD it will be provided." (Genesis 22:14)."I am the LORD, and I do not change. That is why you descendants of Jacob are not already destroyed." (Malachi 3:6).And I know that whatever God does is final. Nothing can be added to it or taken from it. God's purpose is that people should fear him (Ecclesiastes 3:14).

General Confession

There once was a man named Job who lived in the land of Uz. He was blameless — a man of complete integrity. He feared God and stayed away from evil (Job 1: 1).

I decree that all these will be said of me: blameless, man / woman of integrity, man / woman that have the fear of God and man / woman that stay clear of evil.

"But consider the joy of those corrected by God! Do not despise the discipline of the Almighty when you sin. [18] For though he wounds, he also bandages. He strikes, but his hands also heal (Job 5:17-18).

I thank You Lord, for binding my wounds and healing me with your strong arm, in Jesus' name. Amen!

Arise, shine; for thy light is come, and the glory of the Lord is risen upon thee (Isaiah 60:1 KJV).

I decree that my light will continually shine for all to see, in Jesus' name. Amen!

General Confession

For I will pour water upon him that is thirsty, and floods upon the dry ground: I will pour my spirit upon thy seed, and my blessing upon thine offspring: (Isaiah 44:3 KJV).

I thank You Lord for pouring your Spirit upon my seed; the Spirit of excellence and the Spirit of greatness. My children shall be great leaders of their generation. They remain blessed, in Jesus' name. Amen!

For the LORD God is our sun and our shield. He gives us grace and glory. The LORD will withhold no good thing from those who do what is right (Psalm 84:11).

The Lord is gracious to me and my household; He will withhold no good thing from us, we give You praise. Hallelujah!

For with God nothing shall be impossible (Luke 1:37 KJV).

The Lord turns every impossible suituation of my life, and family around, and surprises us with His wondrous acts. Hallelujah!

For thou shalt eat the labour of thine hands: happy shalt thou be, and it shall be well with thee (Psalm 128:2 KJV).

My reward is sure, all my labor shall never be in vain; I will eat the labor of my hands, in Jesus' name. Amen!

Blotting out the handwriting of ordinances that was against us, which was contrary to us, and took it out of the way, nailing it to his cross; [15] And having spoiled principalities and powers, he made a shew of them openly, triumphing over them in it (Colossians 2:14-15 KJV).

The record of charges against me and my household have been cancelled when Jesus was nailed to the cross. Hallelujah, thank You Jesus!

And his mercy is on them that fear him from generation to generation (Luke 1:50 KJV).

The mercy of the Lord is on me and my household from generation to generation, in Jesus' name. Amen!

"If I were you, I would go to God and present my case to him. [9] He does great things too marvelous to understand. He performs countless miracles." (Job 5:8-9).

Almighty God, I know Your strength and might; I know You can do all things, You perform countless miracles. I trust You Lord, my expectations will not be disappointed, in Jesus' name.

Those who trust in the LORD are as secure as Mount Zion; they will not be defeated but will endure forever (Psalm 125:1).

I cannot be defeated because I put my trust in You, together with my household. We are victorious in Christ Jesus. Hallelujah!

Surely there is no enchantment against Jacob, neither is there any divination against Israel: according to this time it shall be said of Jacob and of Israel, What hath God wrought! (Numbers 23:23 KJV).

Replace Jacob with your name and Israel with your family name and confess aloud.

Though hand join in hand, the wicked shall not be unpunished: but the seed of the righteous shall be delivered (Proverbs 11:21 KJV).

The conspiracy of the wicked against my seed will not prosper; my seed shall be delivered.

He disappointeth the devices of the crafty, so that their hands cannot perform their enterprise (Job 5:12 KJV).

The Lord will continually disappoint the devices of the wicked over my life, and the lives of my loved ones, their evil plans will never succeed, in Jesus' name. Amen!

He rescues the poor from the cutting words of the strong, and rescues them from the clutches of the powerful (Job 5:15).

The great deliverer, I give you praise and thank You; only You can deliver totally, You rescue me and my household from the powerful clutches of the wicked. Hallelujah!

You have always put a wall of protection around him and his home and his property. You have made him prosper in everything he does. Look how rich he is! (Job1: 10).

I thank You Lord for the heritage I have in You. You protect those that belong to You; Your wall of protection is all around my household, blessing our home, and the work of our hands.

Just as the mountains surround Jerusalem, so the LORD surrounds his people, both now and forever (Psalm 125:2).

I, and my family dwell in safety at all times; the mighty arms of the Lord surround us. We shall not be moved, in Jesus' name. Amen!

The wicked will not rule the land of the godly, for then the godly might be tempted to do wrong (Psalm 125:3).

I decree Godly leaders for our Nation; leaders that have the fear of God in them, in Jesus' name. Amen!

You will go to the grave at a ripe old age, like a sheaf of grain harvested at the proper time! (Job 5:26).

Long life is my portion and heritage: I will not die young, I will live to reap the rewards of my labor over my children and I will see my children's children in, Jesus' name. Amen!

Praise the LORD! How joyful are those who fear the LORD and delight in obeying his commands. [2] Their children will be successful everywhere; an entire generation of godly people will be blessed (Psalm 112:1-2).

I decree that my children and their children will be great in my lifetime, in Jesus' name. Amen!

General Confession

And Sarah declared, "God has brought me laughter. All who hear about this will laugh with me." (Genesis 21:6).

I thank You Lord for bringing laughter into my life, household; it shall be permanent, in Jesus' name. Amen!

And it shall come to pass in that day, that his burden shall be taken away from off thy shoulder, and his yoke from off thy neck and the yoke shall be destroyed because of the anointing (Isaiah 10:27 KJV).

Every burden, yoke of the devil is taken off my shoulders and neck. I am free from every bondage or oppression of the devil, in Jesus' name. Amen!

But you will receive power when the Holy Spirit comes upon you. And you will be my witnesses, telling people about me everywhere–in Jerusalem, throughout Judea, in Samaria, and to the ends of the earth (Acts 1:8).

I decree that the power of God in me will not lie dormant; I will be an effective soul winner, in Jesus' name. Amen!

Many are the afflictions of the righteous: but the Lord delivereth him out of them all (Psalm 34:19 KJV).

My heavenly Father is more than able to take care of all my afflictions and challenges. He is ever faithful; my deliverance is complete, in Jesus' name. Amen!

So I say, let the Holy Spirit guide your lives. Then you won't be doing what your sinful nature craves (Galatians 5:16).

I submit to the Holy Spirit to guide me, through my everyday decisions. I will not yield to the dictates of my flesh, in Jesus' name. Amen!

For God is working in you, giving you the desire and the power to do what pleases Him (Philippians 2:13).

God is at work in me putting in me a strong desire to please Him; I will do Your will and counsel Lord.

Must we be strung up on their hooks and caught in their nets while they rejoice and celebrate? (Habakkuk 1:15)

I, and my household will not be caught in the net, trap or pit of the wicked, The Spirit of the Lord will order our every step, in Jesus' name. Amen!

For his anger lasts only a moment, but his favor lasts a lifetime! Weeping may last through the night, but joy comes with the morning (Psalm 30:5).

My joy cometh! The favor of the Lord will locate me and my household, the Lord will be gracious unto us, in Jesus' name. Amen!

Don't envy sinners, but always continue to fear the LORD. [18] You will be rewarded for this; your hope will not be disappointed (Proverbs 23:17-18).

My faith in the Lord will not be disappointed, in Jesus' name. Amen!

Stretch out your hand with healing power; may miraculous signs and wonders be done through the name of Your holy servant Jesus (Acts 4:30).

The Lord will stretch forth His hand over me and my household; He'll heal our mortal bodies with miraculous signs and wonders, in Jesus' name. Amen!

Jesus responded, "Didn't I tell you that you would see God's glory if you believe?" (John 11:40).

Lord, I believe. Let me see your glory in every area of my life: my health, work of my hands, and family, in Jesus' name. Amen!

Have not I commanded thee? Be strong and of a good courage; be not afraid, neither be thou dismayed: for the Lord thy God is with thee whithersoever thou goest (Joshua 1:9 KJV).

I thank You Lord, for Your protective arms round about me and my household. I will not be afraid of any: evil, terror, violence, accident, challenge.....

Behold, I and the children whom the Lord hath given me are for signs and for wonders in Israel from the Lord of hosts, which dwelleth in mount Zion (Isaiah 8:18 KJV).

I, and my children are for signs and wonders in this land of the living. We shall be a terror to the kingdom of darkness; doing exploits for the Lord, in Jesus' name. Amen!

My child, pay attention to what I say. Listen carefully to my words. [21] Don't lose sight of them. Let them penetrate deep into your heart, [22] for they bring life to those who find them, and healing to their whole body (Proverbs 4:20-22).

The word of God is my medicine. I decree as I meditate and confess God's word, it will go deep into my heart; bringing life and healing to my whole body, in Jesus' name. Amen!

Therefore, my beloved brethren, be ye stedfast, unmoveable, always abounding in the work of the Lord, forasmuch as ye know that your labour is not in vain in the Lord (1Corinthians 15:58 KJV).

I choose to be steadfast, immoveable, always abounding in the work of the Lord; for I know my labor in His vineyard can never be in vain, in Jesus' name. Amen!

Thy word have I hid in mine heart, that I might not sin against thee (Psalm 119:11).

The Holy Spirit will hinder me from sinning against God; he will always bring the word of God in my heart to my remembrance, in Jesus' name. Amen!

Your word is a lamp to guide my feet and a light for my path (Psalm 119:105).

The word of God will always be my guide, shining along my path; I will not derail, in Jesus' name. Amen!

As the deer longs for streams of water, so I long for you, O God (Psalm 42:1).

The word of God will be my delight day and night; it will be the longing of my soul, in Jesus' name. Amen!

May the words of my mouth and the meditation of my heart be pleasing to you, O LORD, my rock and my redeemer (Psalm 19:14).

I decree that my words, thoughts and actions will always please the Lord, in Jesus' name. Amen!

And so, dear friends, while you are waiting for these things to happen, make every effort to be found living peaceful lives that are pure and blameless in his sight (2 Peter 3:14).

I choose to live a pure, blameless life; living peacefully with every one, even as I await the return of the Lord, in Jesus' name. Amen!

Seest thou a man diligent in business? he shall stand before kings; he shall not stand before mean men (Proverbs 22:29 KJV).

The Lord will order my steps to stand before kings (people that will favor me) and not mean men, in Jesus' name. Amen!

And God will generously provide all you need. Then you will always have everything you need and plenty left over to share with others (2 Corinthians 9:8).

I thank You Lord, for Your grace upon me, and every member of my family; all our needs are met, we give You praise.

Have you never heard? Have you never understood? The LORD is the everlasting God, the Creator of all the earth. He never grows weak or weary. No one can measure the depths of his understanding. [29] He gives power to the weak and strength to the powerless (Isaiah 40:28-29).

I receive new power and strength from the Lord daily; inner and physical strength to keep me going. I cannot be weak or weary, in Jesus' name. Amen!

Christian Growth

I pray that your love will overflow more and more, and that you will keep on growing in knowledge and understanding (Philippians 1:9).

I decree that the love I, and my entire household have for God, will overflow more and more even as we grow deeper in the knowledge and understanding of the Lord, in Jesus' name. Amen!

May you always be filled with the fruit of your salvation the righteous character produced in your life by Jesus Christ for this will bring much glory and praise to God (Philippians 1:11).

I decree, that I will bear fruit in Christ: fruit that can be seen by all, fruit that will give glory and praise to the Almighty, in Jesus' name. Amen!

For God is working in you, giving you the desire and the power to do what pleases him (Philippians 2:13).

The Holy Spirit is at work in me, and every member of my household; giving us the desire and power to please Him in all we do. We choose to please You Lord.

So that no one can criticize you. Live clean, innocent lives as children of God, shining like bright lights in a world full of crooked and perverse people (Philippians 2:15).

I decree that my light will shine continually as I live a clean, innocent life; illuminating this dark world, in Jesus' name. Amen!

For I fully expect and hope that I will never be ashamed, but that I will continue to be bold for Christ, as I have been in the past. And I trust that my life will bring honor to Christ, whether I live or die (Philippians 1:20).

I decree that my life will always honor You: my words, thoughts and deeds. I will continually live for You Lord, bringing glory to Your name, in Jesus' name. Amen!

All the others care only for themselves and not for what matters to Jesus Christ (Philippians 2:21).

I decree that Jesus will be my priority; I receive the strength and grace needed, in Jesus' name. Amen!

So we have not stopped praying for you since we first heard about you. We ask God to give you complete knowledge of his will and to give you spiritual wisdom and understanding. [10] Then the way you live will always honor and please the Lord, and your lives will produce every kind of good fruit. All the while, you will grow as you learn to know God better and better (Colossians 1:9-10).

I receive complete knowledge of Your will, spiritual wisdom and understanding. I decree that my lifestyle will always honor and please the Lord, bearing every kind of good fruit, in Jesus' name. Amen!

And the spirit of the Lord shall rest upon him, the spirit of wisdom and understanding, the spirit of counsel and might, the spirit of knowledge and of the fear of the Lord; (Isaiah 11:2 KJV).

I decree that the same spirit that rested on our Lord Jesus Christ: spirit of wisdom and understanding, spirit of counsel and might, spirit of knowledge and of the fear of the Lord shall rest upon me and every member of my household, in Jesus' name. Amen!

But the path of the just is as the shining light, that shineth more and more unto the perfect day (Proverbs 4:18 KJV).

I decree that my path and that of every member of my household is as the shining light; it will shine brighter and brighter, no darkness will be found along our path, in Jesus' name. Amen!

But you will receive power when the Holy Spirit comes upon you. And you will be my witnesses, telling people about me everywhere–in Jerusalem, throughout Judea, in Samaria, and to the ends of the earth." (Acts 1:8).

The power of God I have in me will not lie dormant; I will be an effective soul winner, in Jesus' name. Amen!

So I say, let the Holy Spirit guide your lives. Then you won't be doing what your sinful nature craves (Galatians 5:16).

I submit to the Holy Spirit to guide me, through my everyday decisions. I will not yield to the dictates of my flesh, in Jesus' name. Amen!

Therefore, my beloved brethren, be ye stedfast, unmoveable, always abounding in the work of the Lord, forasmuch as ye know that your labour is not in vain in the Lord (1 Corinthians 15:58 KJV).

I choose to be steadfast, immoveable, always abounding in the work of the Lord; I will not be discouraged for I know my labor in His vineyard can never be in vain, in Jesus' name. Amen!

Search me, O God, and know my heart; test me and know my anxious thoughts. [24] Point out anything in me that offends you, and lead me along the path of everlasting life (Psalm 139:23-24).

I receive the grace to work on all that displease the Lord in my life, that I may remain in the path of everlasting life, in Jesus' name. Amen!

Thy word have I hid in mine heart, that I might not sin against thee (Psalm 119:11 KJV).

The Holy Spirit will hinder me from sinning against God; He will always bring the word of God in my heart to my remembrance, in Jesus' name. Amen!

As the deer longs for streams of water, so I long for you, O God (Psalm 42:1).
The word of God will be my delight day and night; it will be the longing of my soul, in Jesus' name. Amen!

May the words of my mouth and the meditation of my heart be pleasing to you, O LORD, my rock and my redeemer (Psalm 19:14).
I decree that my words, thoughts and actions will always please the Lord, in Jesus' name. Amen!

And so, dear friends, while you are waiting for these things to happen, make every effort to be found living peaceful lives that are pure and blame less in his sight (2 Peter 3:14).
I choose to live a pure, blameless life; living peacefully with every one, even as I await the return of the Lord, in Jesus' name. Amen!

And the very God of peace sanctify you wholly; and I pray God your whole spirit and soul and body be preserved blameless unto the coming of our Lord Jesus Christ (1Thes 5: 23 KJV).

I thank You Lord for full sanctification of my spirit, soul and body; I decree I remain blameless unto the coming of our Lord Jesus Christ.

For I am persuaded, that neither death, nor life, nor angels, nor principalities, nor powers, nor things present, nor things to come, [39] Nor height, nor depth, nor any other creature, shall be able to separate us from the love of God, which is in Christ Jesus our Lord (Romans 8:38-39 KJV).

I decree that nothing can separate me and my household from the love of God, which is in Christ Jesus. We choose to remain steadfast in our faith, in Jesus' name. Amen!

But you are not like that, for you are a chosen people. You are royal priests, a holy nation, God's very own possession. As a result, you can show others the goodness of God, for he called you out of the darkness into his wonderful light (1 Peter 2:9).

I am God's very own possession I will show others the goodness of God; who has called me out of darkness into His marvelous light.

These were his instructions to them: "The harvest is great, but the workers are few. So pray to the Lord who is in charge of the harvest; ask him to send more workers into his fields (Luke 10:2).

I, and every member of my household, will be part of the harvest in God's vineyard. We will be worthy laborers, in Jesus' name. Amen!

Ask me and I will tell you remarkable secrets you do not know about things to come (Jeremiah 33: 3).

The Lord will reveal the deep secrets about His kingdom to me; I will not be in the dark concerning the future events of my life, in Jesus' name. Amen!

But those who wish to boast should boast in this alone: that they truly know me and understand that I am the lord who demonstrates unfailing love and who brings justice and righteousness to the earth, and that I delight in these things. I, the lord, have spoken! (Jeremiah 9: 24).

My boast will be in my true knowledge and understanding of the Lord Almighty; my longing and craving is for You alone Lord.

Faith

And Abraham's faith did not weaken, even though, at about 100 years of age, he figured his body was as good as dead-and so was Sarah's womb. [20] Abraham never wavered in believing God's promise. In fact, his faith grew stronger, and in this he brought glory to God (Romans 4:19-20).

My faith will remain strong in the Lord, growing by the day; I will not waver in believing God in every aspect of my life, until I see the Lord perform all my expectations, in Jesus' name. Amen!

So be strong and courageous, all you who put your hope in the LORD! (Psalm 31:24).

I receive strength to go through any trial or challenge I may face; by the help of the Holy Spirit, I will be strong through every situation, in Jesus' name. Amen!

Nevertheless my loving-kindness will I not utterly take from him, nor suffer my faithfulness to fail. [34] My covenant will I not break, nor alter the thing that is gone out of my lips (Psalm 89: 33-34 KJV).

Lord, You are a God that keeps promises; Your promises indeed are yea and Amen. You are not a covenant breaker; You surely will perform it by Your faithfulness and loving-kindness, in Jesus' name. Amen!

Mine eyes shall be upon the faithful of the land that they may dwell with me: he that walketh in a perfect way, he shall serve me (Psalm 101:6 KJV).

The eyes of the Lord are upon me: my affairs, my going out and coming in, I shall not be moved.

Then the presidents and princes sought to find occasion against Daniel concerning the kingdom; but they could find none occasion nor fault; forasmuch as he was faithful, neither was there any error or fault found in him (Daniel 6:4 KJV).

I choose to remain faithful and loyal in my service and commitment to God, in Jesus' name. Amen!

Behold, his soul which is lifted up is not upright in him: but the just shall live by his faith (Habakkuk 2:4 KJV).

I decree I will put my faith to work at all times, in Jesus' name. Amen!

Then Jesus answered and said unto her, O woman, great is thy faith: be it unto thee even as thou wilt. And her daughter was made whole from that very hour (Matthew 15:28 KJV).

I decree it will be unto me accordingly to my faith and expectation, in Jesus' name. Amen

They are new every morning: great is thy faithfulness (Lamentations 3:23 KJV).

I appreciate You faithful God, You are always faithful; great is Your faithfulness toward me and every member of my household. Thank You Jesus!

And Jesus answering saith unto them, Have faith in God (Mark 11:22 KJV).

I choose to have faith in God; I come against every doubt or fear, in Jesus' name. Amen!

And the apostles said unto the Lord, Increase our faith (Luke 17:5 KJV).

I decree that henceforth my faith will be on the rise: I will pay more attention on the word of God, pray more and do more spiritual exercise, in Jesus' name. Amen!

But I have pleaded in prayer for you, Simon that your faith should not fail. So when you have repented and turned to me again, strengthen your brothers." (Luke 22:32).

I decree that in the day of adversity my faith in God will be strong; it will not fail, in Jesus' name. Amen!

And the saying pleased the whole multitude: and they chose Stephen, a man full of faith and of the Holy Ghost, and Philip, and Prochorus, and Nicanor, and Timon, and Parmenas, and

Nicolas a proselyte of Antioch: [8] And Stephen, full of faith and power, did great wonders and miracles among the people (Acts 6:5, 8 KJV).

The Lord will make me to be full of faith and power, that I may wrought great wonders and miracles among God's people, in Jesus' name. Amen!

And being fully persuaded that, what he had promised, he was able also to perform (Romans 4:21 KJV).

The Lord will bring to pass all he has promised in accordance to His word; none will fall to the ground, in Jesus' name. Amen!

Be on guard. Stand firm in the faith. Be courageous. Be strong (1 Corinthians 16:13).

I decree to always be on guard, standing firm in the faith; I'll be courageous and strong by the help of the Holy Spirit, in Jesus' name. Amen!

(For we walk by faith, not by sight:) (2 Corinthians 5:7 KJV).

I choose to walk by faith, trusting the Lord all the way, in Jesus' name. Amen!

Faithful is he that calleth you, who also will do it (1 Thessalonians 5:24 KJV).

My Savior is a faithful God, He has not called me into shame or reproach; He will bring to pass all my expectations, none of my expectations will be disappointed, in Jesus' name. Amen!

But let him ask in faith, nothing wavering. For he that wavereth is like a wave of the sea driven with the wind and tossed (James 1:6 KJV).

I choose not to waver in my faith, I know in whom I believe; He is a faithful God.

But I am like an olive tree, thriving in the house of God. I will always trust in God's unfailing love (Psalm 52:8).

Lord, I know your unfailing love is real; I will pull through these, in Jesus' name. Amen!

Trust ye in the Lord for ever: for in the Lord Jehovah is everlasting strength: (Isaiah 26: 4 KJV).

Lord, I trust in your everlasting Strength; the same strength that parted the red sea, for the children of Israel to pass through, is at work in my situation. I will not fear.

Who art thou, O great mountain? before Zerubbabel thou shalt become a plain: and he shall bring forth the headstone thereof with shoutings, crying , Grace, grace unto it (Zechariah 4:7 KJV).

I command every mountain before me: mountain of sickness, lack, disability, fear.... to become a plain; not by my power or might but by Your Spirit, oh Lord.

Trust in the LORD with all your heart; do not depend on your own understanding. [6] Seek his will in all you do, and he will show you which path to take (Proverbs 3:5-6).

I choose to seek Your will in all I do, trusting and depending on You; I know You will lead me in the right path, in Jesus' name. Amen!

I will wait for the LORD, who has turned away from the descendants of Jacob. I will put my hope in him (Isaiah 8:17).

I receive all the strength I need to wait on You Lord, in Jesus' name. Amen!

Don't envy sinners, but always continue to fear the LORD. [18] You will be rewarded for this; your hope will not be disappointed (Proverbs 23:17-18).

I put my whole Faith in You Lord; You will surely reward me, for You are a rewarder of those who diligently seek You. You will honor my faith, in Jesus' name. Amen!

Jesus responded, "Didn't I tell you that you would see God's glory if you believe?" (John 11:40).

I believe Lord; let me see your glory in every area of my life: my health, work of my hands, and my family in Jesus' name. Amen!

"Don't let your hearts be troubled. Trust n Him, and trust also in me (John 14:1).

My heart will not be troubled, He that made the heaven and the earth is on my side; I will not be moved, in Jesus' name. Amen!

Why am I discouraged? Why is my heart so sad? I will put my hope in Him! I will praise him again- my Savior and my God! (Psalm 43:5).

I will not be discouraged or sad, my God is enthroned forever; I will put my hope in God, He is faithful. Hallelujah!

Don't be afraid, for I am with you. Don't be discouraged, for I am your God. I will strengthen you and help you. I will hold you up with my victorious right hand (Isaiah 41: 10).

The Lord holds me, and my household up with His victorious right hand; we will not be afraid or discouraged. God will surely help us, in Jesus' name. Amen!

Wherefore also it is contained in the scripture, Behold, I lay in Sion a chief corner stone, elect, precious: and he that believeth on him shall not be confounded (1 Peter 2:6 KJV).

I believe in God, I will not be put to shame, in Jesus' name. Amen!

"You don't have enough faith," Jesus told them. "I tell you the truth, if you had faith even as small as a mustard seed, you could say to this mountain, 'Move from here to there,' and it would move. Nothing would be impossible." (Matthew 17:20).

I command a turn around in every adverse situation of my life, in Jesus' name. Amen!

Thou shalt also decree a thing, and it shall be established unto thee: and the light shall shine upon thy ways (Job 22: 28 KJV).

Begin to decree your entire expectations one after the other........ They will surely come to pass, in Jesus' name. Amen!

Better is the end of a thing than the beginning thereof: and the patient in spirit is better than the proud in spirit (Ecclesiastes 7: 8 KJV).

I receive the grace to wait patiently on You Lord, I know my tomorrow will be good and joyous, in Jesus' name. Amen!

When Jesus woke up, he rebuked the wind and said to the waves, "Silence! Be still!" Suddenly the wind stopped, and there was a great calm. [40] Then he asked them, "Why are you afraid? Do you still have no faith?" (Mark 4:39-40).

I rebuke every contrary wind blowing against me and every member of my family; I decree a great calm, in Jesus' name. Amen!

Those who look to him for help will be radiant with joy; no shadow of shame will darken their faces (Psalm 34:5).

My God is the Almighty, as I look on Him for help, I will radiate with Joy in Jesus' name. Amen!

Deliverance / Warfare

He delivereth me from mine enemies: yea, thou liftest me up above those that rise up against me: thou hast delivered me from the violent man (Psalm 18:48 KJV).
I give You praise Lord for delivering me from the violet man; my God is mighty in battle.

They cried out to you and were saved. They trusted in you and were never disgraced (Psalm 22:5).
God is my saving grace; I can never be disgraced, for surely the Lord will arise on my behalf.

There is no king saved by the multitude of an host: a mighty man is not delivered by much strength (Psalm 33:16 KJV).
My strength is small Lord. I turn over every battle of my life to You; You have never lost a battle, I give you praise. Hallelujah!

Deliverance / Warfare

Behold, the eye of the Lord is upon them that fear him, upon them that hope in his mercy; [19] To deliver their soul from death, and to keep them alive in famine (Psalm 33:18-19 KJV).

The eye of the Lord is upon me, my household, to deliver our souls from death, and keep us alive in famine, in Jesus' name. Amen!

Shall the prey be taken from the mighty, or the lawful captive delivered?
[25] But thus saith the Lord, Even the captives of the mighty shall be taken away, and the prey of the terrible shall be delivered: for I will contend with him that contendeth with thee, and I will save thy children (Isaiah 49:24-25 KJV).

Thank You Lord for contending with every force that contend with me and my household; our deliverance is sure, in Jesus' name. Amen!

[6] This poor man cried, and the Lord heard him, and saved him out of all his troubles (Psalm34:6).

Helper of the helpless, I give you praise; thank You for saving me from all my troubles.

[7] The angel of the Lord encampeth round about them that fear him, and delivereth them (Psalm 34:7 KJV).

Thank You Lord for Your angelic protection, they're always alert to deliver me. Hallelujah!

And it shall come to pass, that whosoever shall call on the name of the Lord shall be delivered: for in mount Zion and in Jerusalem shall be deliverance, as the Lord hath said, and in the remnant whom the Lord shall call (Joel 2:32 KJV).

I receive total deliverance for myself, and every member of my household, in Jesus' name Amen!

Though hand join in hand, the wicked shall not be unpunished: but the seed of the righteous shall be delivered (Proverbs 11:21 KJV).

My seed is preserved; no wicked plan of the devil will ever prosper in their lives, in Jesus' name Amen!

For you have rescued me from death; you have kept my feet from slipping. So now I can walk in your presence, O God, in your life-giving light (Psalm 56:13).

Thank You Lord, for rescuing me from the spirit of death; it could not prevail over me. You kept my feet from slipping, Lord I give You praise. Hallelujah!

Rescue me from the mud; don't let me sink any deeper! Save me from those who hate me, and pull me from these deep waters (Psalm 69:14).

My God is my sure support, I will not sink; He's more than able to preserve me from sinking. Hallelujah!

He sent out his word and healed them, snatching them from the door of death (Psalm 107:20).

Almighty father, Your word on my lips brings me deliverance; renew my strength daily in this battle, that I may be completely victorious, in Jesus' name. Amen!

When Ahaz, son of Jotham and grandson of Uzziah, was king of Judah, King Rezin of Syria and Pekah son of Remaliah, the king of Israel, set out to attack Jerusalem. However, they were unable to carry out their plan (Isaiah 7: 1).

My enemies cannot carry out their plans against me and my household; there will always be confusion in their camp, in Jesus' name. Amen!

But this is what the Sovereign LORD says: "This invasion will never happen; it will never take place; (Isaiah 7:7).

I forbid any form of invasion against me or any member of my household; it will never happen, in Jesus' name. Amen!

Israel is no stronger than its capital, Samaria, and Samaria is no stronger than its king, Pekah son of Remaliah. Unless your faith is firm, I cannot make you stand firm." (Isaiah 7:9).

My faith is firm, that no plan or conspiracy of the wicked against: me, my household, my Church and my nation will ever stand, in Jesus' name. Amen!

And it shall come to pass in that day, that his burden shall be taken away from off thy shoulder, and his yoke from off thy neck, and the yoke shall be destroyed because of the anointing (Isaiah 10:27 KJV).

I destroy, whatever burden or yoke the devil has laid on me, or any member of my family, by the power of the Holy Ghost, in Jesus' name. Amen!

But the LORD stands beside me like a great warrior. Before him my persecutors will stumble. They cannot defeat me. They will fail and be thoroughly humiliated. Their dishonor will never be forgotten (Jeremiah 20:11).

The Lord of host is standing with me in battle, my persecutors will stumble and fail; they cannot prevail, in Jesus' name. Amen!

Many are the afflictions of the righteous: but the Lord delivereth him out of them all (Psalm 34:19 KJV).

The afflictions of my life may be many, but the Lord of host will deliver me out of them all. Total victory is my portion in Jesus name. Amen!

Must we be strung up on their hooks and caught in their nets while they rejoice and celebrate? (Habakkuk 1:15).

I, my household will not be caught in the net of the wicked; the Spirit of the Lord will guide our every step, in Jesus' name. Amen!

So you see, the Lord knows how to rescue godly people from their trials, even while keeping the wicked under punishment until the day of final judgment (2 Peter 2:9).

The Lord will rescue me, my household from every trial we may face; we will not be defeated in Jesus' name. Amen!

But I am poor and needy: make haste unto me, O God: thou art my help and my deliverer; O Lord, make no tarrying (Psalm 70:5 KJV).

I await your help and deliverance oh Lord, do not let me down.

He rescues the poor from the cutting words of the strong, and rescues them from the clutches of the powerful (Job 5:15).

Almighty God, only You can rescue, only You can save; thank You for saving me from the grip of the powerful.

He disappointeth the devices of the crafty, so that their hands cannot perform their enterprise (Job 5:12 KJV).

Lord, You will forever disappoint the devices of the crafty, so their hands cannot perform their enterprise.

From six disasters he will rescue you; even in the seventh, he will keep you from evil (Job 5:19).

Great deliverer, I thank You for Your divine intervention in every battle of my life.

You will go to the grave at a ripe old age, like a sheaf of grain harvested at the proper time! (Job 5:26).

I will go to the grave at a ripe old age, like a sheaf of grain harvested at the proper time! I will live to fulfill my destiny; I will not be cut short, in Jesus' name. Amen!

Because you trusted me, I will give you your life as a reward. I will rescue you and keep you safe. I, the LORD, have spoken!'" (Jeremiah 39:18).

I thank You Lord, for restoring my life back to me; great deliverer, I give You praise.

You gave me victory over my accusers. You appointed me ruler over nations; people I don't even know now serve me (Psalm 18:43).

I have victory over my accusers, Your mercy always override judgment in my life. I thank You Jesus.

Now know I that the Lord saveth his anointed; he will hear him from his holy heaven with the saving strength of his right hand (Psalm 20:6 KJV).

I trust in the saving strength of Your right hand Lord; You will cause all oppression in my life to cease, in Jesus' name. Amen!

Deliverance / Warfare

Pull me out of the net that they have laid privily for me: for thou art my strength (Psalm 31:4 KJV).

Lord, pull me and my family out of every net or trap laid secretly for us, in Jesus' name. Amen!

There is no king saved by the multitude of a host: a mighty man is not delivered by much strength. [17] An horse is a vain thing for safety: neither shall he deliver any by his great strength (Psalm 33:16-17 KJV).

But the salvation of the righteous is of the Lord: he is their strength in the time of trouble. [40] And the Lord shall help them, and deliver them: he shall deliver them from the wicked, and save them, because they trust in him (Psalm 37:39-40 KJV).

The help of man is in vain. You're my sure help Lord, in You I put my trust; You will surely deliver me.

For I hold you by your right hand— I, the lord your God. And I say to you, 'Don't be afraid. I am here to help you. You will be a new threshing instrument with many sharp teeth. You will tear your enemies apart, making chaff of mountains (Isaiah 41:13-15).

You made me like a new threshing instrument with many teeth; You've made me effective in warfare, thank You Jesus.

They are ashamed and confounded that seek after my soul: They are turned backward, and put to confusion, that desire my hurt (Psalm 70:2 KJV).

Let them be ashamed and confounded that seek after my soul, and the soul of any member of my family: let them be turned backward, and put to confusion, that desire our hurt, in Jesus' name. Amen!

And Jesus said unto them, Because of your unbelief: for verily I say unto you, If ye have faith as a grain of mustard seed, ye shall say unto this mountain, Remove hence to yonder place; and it shall remove; and nothing shall be impossible unto you (Matthew 17:20 KJV).

I command every mountain along my path: mountain of fear, difficulty, unbelief, impossibilities, sickness, failure, lack………..to level, in Jesus' name. Amen!

Let the sighing of the prisoner come before thee; according to the greatness of thy power preserve thou those that are appointed to die; (Psalm 79:11 KJV).

I thank You Lord, for reversing every death sentence that may be lingering over my life or life of any member of my household, in Jesus' name. Amen!

The LORD of Heaven's Armies has spoken- who can change his plans? When his hand is raised, who can stop him?" (Isaiah 14:27).

God's counsel will prevail in my life, and the life of every member of my family, in Jesus' name. Amen!

Deliverance / Warfare

Seeing it is a righteous thing with God to recompense tribulation to them that trouble you; (2 Thessalonians 1:6 KJV).

I am God's divine property; God repays tribulation to all that trouble me.

The enemy shall not exact upon him; nor the son of wickedness afflict him. [23] And I will beat down his foes before his face, and plague them that hate him (Psalm 89:22-23 KJV).

God will not allow my enemies to defeat or overpower me; He will beat them down and plague them.

But, O Lord of hosts, that triest the righteous, and seest the reins and the heart, let me see thy vengeance on them: for unto thee have I opened my cause (Jeremiah 20:12 KJV).

God will avenge, everyone that rise against me and my household, in Jesus' name. Amen!

And the Lord shall deliver me from every evil work, and will preserve me unto his heavenly kingdom: to whom be glory for ever and ever. Amen (2 Timothy 4:18 KJV).

God will deliver me from every evil attack, and will bring me safely into his heavenly Kingdom. All glory to God forever and ever. Amen!

And he said, Open the window eastward. And he opened it. Then Elisha said, Shoot. And he shot. And he said, The arrow of the Lord's deliverance, and the arrow of deliverance from Syria: for thou shalt smite the Syrians in Aphek, till thou have consumed them (2 Kings 13:17 KJV).

The arrow of the Lord's Deliverance will locate every satanic force, which rise against me and my household, in Jesus' name. Amen!

The LORD replies, "I have seen violence done to the helpless, and I have heard the groans of the poor. Now I will rise up to rescue them, as they have longed for me to do." (Psalm 12:5).

I thank You Lord for rising up to my rescue, in Jesus' name. Amen!

Fear

For I hold you by your right hand- I, the LORD your God. And I say to you, 'Don't be afraid. I am here to help you (Isaiah 41:13).
I will not be afraid; the Lord my God will help me.

So that we may boldly say, The Lord is my helper, and I will not fear what man shall do unto me (Hebrews 13:6 KJV).
I boldly say, the Lord is my helper; I will not fear, what man shall do unto me. Hallelujah!

For, when we were come into Macedonia, our flesh had no rest, but we were troubled on every side; without were fightings, within were fears… (2 Corinthians 7:5 KJV).
Lord I commit my inner fears unto you; take charge.

For God hath not given us the spirit of fear; but of power, and of love, and of a sound mind (2 Timothy 1:7 KJV).

God hath not given me the spirit of fear; but of power, and of love, and of a sound mind. I will not be afraid.

For ye have not received the spirit of bondage again to fear; but ye have received the Spirit of adoption, whereby we cry, Abba, Father. [16] The Spirit itself beareth witness with our spirit, that we are the children of God (Romans 8:15-16 KJV).
I have received the spirit of adoption, whereby I cry, Abba, Father.

I sought the Lord, and he heard me, and delivered me from all my fears (Psalm 34:4 KJV).
I thank You Lord, for delivering me from all my fears. Name them……..

And Joshua said unto them, Fear not, nor be dismayed, be strong and of good courage: for thus shall the Lord do to all your enemies against whom ye fight (Joshua 10:25 KJV).
I am strong and courageous; the Lord will fight for me. He will destroy all my enemies, in Jesus' name. Amen!

And he answered, Fear not: for they that be with us are more than they that be with them (2 Kings 6:16 KJV).
I will not fear; the host of heaven is with me.

And the covenant that I have made with you ye shall not forget; neither shall ye fear other gods. (2 Kings 17:38 KJV).

I thank You Lord for the covenant I made with You; covenant of the blood of Jesus. I shall not fear other gods, in Jesus' name. Amen!

Though a mighty army surrounds me, my heart will not be afraid. Even if I am attacked, I will remain confident (Psalm 27:3).

My confidence is in the Lord I shall not fear any opposition.

God is in the midst of her; she shall not be moved: God shall help her, and that right early (Psalm 46:5 KJV).

God is in the midst of me I shall not be moved. His help will not be late, in Jesus' name. Amen!

Say to them that are of a fearful heart, Be strong, fear not: behold, your God will come with vengeance, even God with a recompence; he will come and save you (Isaiah 35:4 KJV).

My God will come with vengeance; He will come and save me, my heart will not fear.

"Don't be afraid," he said, "for you are very precious to God. Peace! Be encouraged! Be strong!" As he spoke these words to me, I suddenly felt stronger and said to him, "Please speak to me, my lord, for you have strengthened me." (Daniel 10:19).

Your word always give me strength: I'm strong, encouraged and peaceful. Hallelujah!

There is no fear in love; but perfect love casteth out fear: because fear hath torment. He that feareth is not made perfect in love (1 John 4:18 KJV).

I have experienced Your perfect love, therefore I will not fear.

But when Jesus heard it, he answered him, saying, Fear not: believe only, and she shall be made whole (Luke 8:50 KJV).

I put my faith to work; I know the Lord will see me through, in Jesus' name. Amen!

Then he said, "Don't be afraid, Daniel. Since the first day you began to pray for understanding and to humble yourself before your God, your request has been heard in heaven. I have come in answer to your prayer (Daniel 10:12).

Lord Almighty, I'm at peace, I know You have granted my request.

But for twenty-one days the spirit prince of the kingdom of Persia blocked my way. Then Michael, one of the archangels, came to help me, and I left him there with the spirit prince of the kingdom of Persia (Daniel 10:13).

Any foul spirit blocking my Blessing shall be removed by God's archangel in Jesus name. Amen!

Fear not, O land; be glad and rejoice: for the Lord will do great things (Joel 2:21 KJV).

Fear not (your name) for the Lord will do great things. Hallelujah!

Provision

T he LORD is my shepherd; I have all that I need (Psalm 23:1). The needs of my household and Church family are met, in Jesus' name. Amen!

No good thing will he withhold from them that walk uprightly (Psalm 84:11b KJV).
The Lord is my shepherd; I and my household have all that we need. All our needs are met; we shall lack no good thing, in Jesus' name. Amen!

Once I was young, and now I am old. Yet I have never seen the godly abandoned or their children begging for bread (Psalm 37:25).
Lord, in Your faithfulness, You do not abandon Your elect nor allow them go hungry. You are ever sufficient. Hallelujah!

Provision

Abraham named the place Yahweh-Yireh (which means "the lord will provide"). To this day, people still use that name as a proverb: "On the mountain of the lord it will be provided." (Gen.22:14).

My God makes provision available, for me and my household; we shall not lack, in Jesus' name. Amen!

And this same God who takes care of me will supply all your needs from his glorious riches, which have been given to us in Christ Jesus (Philippians 4:19).

My needs and that of my entire family are met, from Christ's glorious riches. Hallelujah!

The silver is mine, and the gold is mine, saith the Lord of hosts (Hag.2: 8.KJV).

I receive all the resources needed in my household, in Jesus' name. Amen!

It is not that we think we are qualified to do anything on our own. Our qualification comes from God (2 Corinthians 3:5).

I receive enabling grace to perform the tasks ahead of me today and always, in Jesus' name. Amen!

And God will generously provide all you need. Then you will always have everything you need and plenty left over to share with others (2 Corinthians 9:8).

I thank You Lord, for Your abundant grace upon me and my family, out of our abundance we will extend to the needy, in Jesus' name. Amen!

Yes, there will be an abundance of flowers and singing and joy! The deserts will become as green as the mountains of Lebanon, as lovely as Mount Carmel or the plain of Sharon. There the LORD will display his glory, the splendor of our God (Isaiah 35:2).

I decree that my life will flourish and blossom; the glory and splendor of the Lord will be evident in my life, in Jesus name. Amen!

Now unto him that is able to do exceeding abundantly above all that we ask or think, according to the power that worketh in us, (Ephesians 3:20 KJV).

I give You praise Lord, for I know You will do beyond what I ask or think, in Jesus' name. Amen!

The righteous shall flourish like the palm tree: he shall grow like a cedar in Lebanon (Psalm 92:12 -14 KJV).

I decree I shall flourish like a palm tree and grow like a cedar in Lebanon, in Jesus' name Amen!

When you see these things, your heart will rejoice. You will flourish like the grass! Everyone will see the Lord's hand of blessing on his servants- and his anger against his enemies (Isaiah 66:14).

The Lord's hand of blessing will be seen upon my life, and the life of every member of my family, in Jesus' name. Amen!

And all the trees will know that it is I, the LORD, who cuts the tall tree down and makes the short tree grow tall. It is I who makes the green tree wither and gives the dead tree new life. I, the LORD, have spoken, and I will do what I said!" (Ezekiel 17:24).

The breath of the Lord is on the work of my hands: my job, career, and business; so I decree constant growth and progress, in Jesus' name Amen!

For promotion cometh neither from the east, nor from the west, nor from the south. [7] But God is the judge: he putteth down one, and setteth up another. [10] All the horns of the wicked also will I cut off; but the horns of the righteous shall be exalted (Psalm 75:6-7, 10 KJV).

The Lord Almighty that lifts and exalt, will promote me beyond my imagination, in Jesus' name Amen!

This book of the law shall not depart out of thy mouth; but thou shalt meditate therein day and night, that thou mayest observe to do according to all that is written therein: for then thou shalt make thy way prosperous, and then thou shalt have good success (Joshua 1:8 KJV).

My way shall be prosperous, as I meditate and speak Your word over my life, in Jesus' name Amen!

Blessed am I that walk not in the counsel of the ungodly, nor stand in the way of sinners, nor sit in the seat of the scornful. [2] But my delight is in the law of the Lord ; and in God's law do I meditate day and night. [3] And I shall be like a tree planted by the rivers of water, that bring forth his fruit in his season; my leaf also shall not wither; and whatsoever I do shall prosper (Psalm 1:1-3 NKJV) personalized.

Save now, I beseech thee, O Lord: O Lord, I beseech thee, send now prosperity (Psalm 118:25 KJV).
Oh Lord, I receive prosperity by your saving hand, in Jesus' name. Amen!

And the children of Israel were fruitful, and increased abundantly, and multiplied, and waxed exceeding mighty; and the land was filled with them (Exodus 1:7 KJV).
I decree fruitfulness, increase, and multiplication over my life, in Jesus' name. Amen!

Though my beginning was small, yet my latter end shall greatly increase (Job 8:7 KJV).
My beginning may be small but I have confidence that my latter end will greatly increase, in Jesus' name. Amen!

Thou shalt increase my greatness, and comfort me on every side (Psalm 71:21 KJV).
The Lord my God shall increase my greatness and comfort me on every side in Jesus' name. Amen!

He will bless them that fear the Lord, both small and great. [14] The Lord shall increase you more and more, you and your children (Psalm 115:13-14 KJV).

The Lord's hand is upon me and generations after me; we shall increase more and more, in Jesus' name. Amen!

Seest thou a man diligent in his business? he shall stand before kings; he shall not stand before mean men (Proverbs 22:29 KJV).

The Lord will order my steps, to stand before kings and not mean men, in Jesus' name. Amen!

You crown the year with a bountiful harvest; even the hard pathways overflow with abundance (Psalm 65:11).

My God crown my year with a bountiful harvest; even the hard pathways overflow with abundance. Hallelujah!

For thus saith the Lord God of Israel, The barrel of meal shall not waste, neither shall the cruse of oil fail, until the day that the Lord sendeth rain upon the earth (1 Kings 17:14 KJV).

I decree that even in famine I shall flourish and not lack supply, in Jesus' name. Amen!

I will open rivers in high places, and fountains in the midst of the valleys: I will make the wilderness a pool of water, and the dry land springs of water (Isaiah 41:19 NKJV).

I decree an overflow over my life, my God shall meet every need of my life abundantly, in Jesus' name. Amen!

They are like trees planted along a riverbank, with roots that reach deep into the water. Such trees are not bothered by the heat or worried by long months of drought. Their leaves stay green, and they never stop producing fruit (Jeremiah 17:8).

Thank You Lord for I know that even in the midst of drought I shall flourish and be fruitful, in Jesus' name. Amen!

Healing

Is there no balm in Gilead; is there no physician there? why then is not the health of the daughter of my people recovered? (Jeremiah 8:22 KJV).

The healing power in the word of God is my medicine; as I confess it I'm made whole, in Jesus' name. Amen!

"But for you who fear my name, the Sun of Righteousness will rise with healing in his wings. And you will go free, leaping with joy like calves let out to pasture (Malachi 4:2).

The Sun of righteousness shall arise with healing in his wings, and I will go forth leaping with Joy, in Jesus' name. Amen!

Jesus realized at once that healing power had gone out from him, so he turned around in the crowd and asked, "Who touched my robe?" (Mark 5:30).

The healing virtue in the word of God is at work in me, as I touch the helm of His garment through my confession, in Jesus' name. Amen!

Stretch out your hand with healing power; may miraculous signs and wonders be done through the name of your holy servant Jesus (Acts 4:30).

The Lord's hand is over me and my household, healing our mortal bodies with miraculous signs and wonders, in Jesus' name. Amen!

How God anointed Jesus of Nazareth with the Holy Ghost and with power: who went about doing good, and healing all that were oppressed of the devil; for God was with him (Acts 10:38 KJV).

The healing virtue of the Lord is at work in me, healing me of every infirmity, in Jesus' name. Amen!

My child, pay attention to what I say. Listen carefully to my words. [21] Don't lose sight of them. Let them penetrate deep into your heart, [22] for they bring life to those who find them, and healing to their whole body (Proverbs 4:20-22).

The word of God is my medicine. I decree as I meditate and confess God's word, it will go deep into my heart; bringing life and healing to my whole body, in Jesus' name. Amen!

Look now; I myself am he! There is no other god but me! I am the one who kills and gives life; I am the one who wounds and heals; no one can be rescued from my powerful hand! (Deuteronomy 32:39).

The Lord heals me of all my wounds; He gives life to my mortal bodies. Hallelujah!

Healing

"I will give you back your health and heal your wounds," says the LORD (Jeremiah 30:17).

I thank You Lord for giving me back my health and healing my wounds, in Jesus' name. Amen!

"But if an angel from heaven appears- a special messenger to intercede for a person and declare that he is upright- he will be gracious and say, 'Rescue him from the grave, for I have found a ransom for his life.' [25] Then his body will become as healthy as a child's, firm and youthful again (Job 33:23-25).

I thank You Lord for rescuing me from the grave; You found a ransom in Your son Jesus Christ for me. Hallelujah!

But he was wounded for our transgressions, he was bruised for our iniquities: the chastisement of our peace was upon him; and with his stripes we are healed (Isaiah 53:5 KJV).

Jesus was wounded for my transgression, bruised for my iniquity, the chastisement of my peace was upon Him; by His stripes I am healed. I thank You Jesus.

He healeth the broken in heart, and bindeth up their wounds (Psalm 147:3 KJV).

I thank You Lord, for binding up my wounds, in Jesus' name. Amen!

Know ye not that ye are the temple of God, and that the Spirit of God dwelleth in you? (1 Corinthians 3:16 KJV)

My Body is the temple of the Holy Spirit; therefore sickness cannot dwell in me, in Jesus' name. Amen!

Who forgiveth all thine iniquities; who healeth all thy diseases; (Psalm 103:3 KJV).

Lord, You forgive all my sins, heal all my diseases. I thank You.

And said, If thou wilt diligently hearken to the voice of the Lord thy God, and wilt do that which is right in his sight, and wilt give ear to his commandments, and keep all his statutes, I will put none of these diseases upon thee, which I have brought upon the Egyptians: for I am the Lord that healeth thee (Exodus 15:26 KJV).

Disease of Egypt cannot be found in me or any member of my family. It shall be unto us according to Your word, in Jesus' name. Amen!

And Jesus went about all Galilee, teaching in their synagogues, and preaching the gospel of the kingdom, and healing all manner of sickness and all manner of disease among the people (Matthew 4:23 KJV).

I thank You Lord for healing me of all manner of sickness, and all manner of disease, in Jesus' name. Amen!

Healing

And the Lord will take away from thee all sickness, and will put none of the evil diseases of Egypt, which thou knowest, upon thee; but will lay them upon all them that hate thee (Deuteronomy 7:15 KJV).

I thank You Lord for taking away from me and my household all sicknesses, all evil diseases, in Jesus' name. Amen!

But he answered and said, every plant, which my heavenly Jesus hath not planted, shall be rooted up (Matthew 15:13 KJV).

I decree that every plant, which my heavenly Father hath not planted in my life, shall be rooted up; by the power of the Holy Ghost, in Jesus' name. Amen!

I will praise thee; for I am fearfully and wonderfully made: marvellous are thy works; and that my soul knoweth right well (Psalm 139:14 KJV).

I decree that I and every member of my household are fearfully and wonderfully made: every cell, tissue, organ of our bodies functions perfectly well, in Jesus' name. Amen!

This fulfilled the word of the Lord through the prophet Isaiah, who said, "He took our sicknesses and removed our diseases." (Matthew 8:17).

I thank You Lord for taking away my sicknesses, and removing all my diseases. Hallelujah!

Remove from me reproach and contempt; for I have kept thy testimonies (Psalm 119:22 KJV).

I thank You Lord for removing every reproach from my life, in Jesus' name. Amen!

But Jesus turned him about, and when he saw her, he said, Daughter, be of good comfort; thy faith hath made thee whole. And the woman was made whole from that hour (Matthew 9:22 KJV).

I thank You Lord for making me whole from the top of my head to the soles of my feet. Hallelujah!

When Jesus saw him lie, and knew that he had been now a long time in that case , he saith unto him, Wilt thou be made whole? (John 5:6 KJV).

I choose to be whole; heal me by your strong arm Lord.

For as the Father raiseth up the dead, and quickeneth them ; even so the Son quickeneth whom he will (John 5:21 KJV).

I thank You father for quickening me. I receive a quickening in every part of my body, in Jesus' name. Amen!

It is the spirit that quickeneth; the flesh profiteth nothing: the words that I speak unto you, they are spirit, and they are life (John 6:63 KJV).

God's words are Spirit and they are life; as I confess it, I know God's quickening power is released, in Jesus' name. Amen!

Healing

(As it is written, I have made thee a father of many nations,) before him whom he believed, even God, who quickeneth the dead, and calleth those things which be not as though they were (Romans 4:17 KJV).

My God quickened the dead; thank You Lord for quickening every dead part in me, in Jesus' name. Amen!

But if the Spirit of him that raised up Jesus from the dead dwell in you, he that raised up Christ from the dead shall also quicken your mortal bodies by his Spirit that dwelleth in you (Romans 8:11 KJV).

The same Spirit that raised Jesus from the dead dwells in me; therefore my mortal bodies are quickened, in Jesus' name. Amen!

And so it is written, the first man Adam was made a living soul; the last Adam was made a quickening spirit (1 Corinthians 15:45 KJV).

Jesus is that quickening Spirit, and He dwells in me. Hallelujah!

Right away a woman who had heard about him came and fell at his feet. Her little girl was possessed by an evil spirit, [26] and she begged him to cast out the demon from her daughter. Since she was a Gentile, born in Syrian Phoenicia, [27] Jesus told her, "First I should feed the children-my own family, the Jews. It isn't right to take food from the children and throw it to the dogs." (Mark 7:25-27).

Healing, deliverance is the children's bread (heritage); I eat my bread and I'm satisfied, in Jesus' name. Amen!

Dear friend, I hope all is well with you and that you are as healthy in body as you are strong in spirit (3 John 1:2).

I thank You Lord for a total well being (spirit, soul and body) for me, and every member of my family.

And he certainly was ill; in fact, he almost died. But God had mercy on him-and also on me, so that I would not have one sorrow after another (Philippians 2:27).

Lord, Your mercy will prevail in the life of my loved ones; I will not sorrow over any one of them, in Jesus' name. Amen!

For though he wounds, he also bandages. He strikes, but his hands also heal (Job 5:18).

I thank You Jesus, for your healing hand over me and every member of my family, in Jesus' name. Amen!

Heal me, O Lord , and I shall be healed; save me, and I shall be saved: for thou art my praise (Jeremiah 17:14 KJV).

I receive my healing, in Jesus' name. Amen!

For even the Son of man came not to be ministered unto, but to minister, and to give his life a ransom for many (Mark 10:45 KJV).

I thank You Lord, for giving Your life as a ransom for me.

Healing

I shall not die, but live, and declare the works of the Lord (Psalm 118:17 KJV).

I decree I shall not die, but live, to declare God's wondrous works, in the land of the living, in Jesus' name. Amen!

For I am the Lord, I change not; therefore ye sons of Jacob are not consumed (Malachi 3:6 KJV).

My God has not changed; He is still a miracle worker.

Touching the Almighty, we cannot find him out: he is excellent in power, and in judgment, and in plenty of justice: he will not afflict (Job 37:23 KJV).

God is excellent in power there's no ailment too complex for Him. I thank You Lord, for making me whole.

He sent out his word and healed them, snatching them from the door of death (Psalm 107:20).

Your life giving word has snatched me from the door of death. Hallelujah!

"Then your salvation will come like the dawn, and your wounds will quickly heal. Your godliness will lead you forward, and the glory of the LORD will protect you from behind (Isaiah 58:8 NLT).

I thank You Lord for quick recovery, in Jesus' name. Amen!

For he hath looked down from the height of his sanctuary; from heaven did the Lord behold the earth; [20] To hear the groaning of the prisoner; to loose those that are appointed to death;

Psalm 102:19-20 KJV

I thank You Lord for hearing my groaning, and reversing every death sentence lingering over me, or any member of my household, in Jesus' name. Amen!

Protection

Love the LORD, all you godly ones! For the LORD protects those who are loyal to him, but he harshly punishes the arrogant (Psalm 31:23).

I decree that my Love and loyalty to the Lord will be on the rise, in Jesus' name. Amen!

No weapon that is formed against thee shall prosper; and every tongue that shall rise against thee in judgment thou shalt condemn. This is the heritage of the servants of the Lord , and their righteousness is of me, saith the Lord (Isaiah 54:17 KJV).

I decree that no weapon formed against: me, my family, my Church shall ever prosper, in Jesus name. Amen!

You need not be afraid of sudden disaster or the destruction that comes upon the wicked, [26] for the LORD is your security. He will keep your foot from being caught in a trap (Proverbs 3:25-26).

I'm secure in the Lord; He keeps my feet from every satanic trap. Hallelujah!

But let all who take refuge in you rejoice; let them sing joyful praises forever. Spread your protection over them, that all who love your name may be filled with joy (Psalm 5:11).

I decree that my joy shall know no bounds; I will forever sing joyful praises of my Lord and King, in Jesus' name. Amen!

Have not I commanded thee? Be strong and of a good courage; be not afraid, neither be thou dismayed: for the Lord thy God is with thee whithersoever thou goest (Joshua 1:9 KJV).

I thank You Lord for your protective arms around me and every member of my household. I will not be afraid of any: evil, terror, violence, accident challenge.....

Be my rock of safety where I can always hide. Give the order to save me, for you are my rock and my fortress (Psalm 71:3).

My God will always be my rock of safety, in Jesus' name. Amen!

Some time later, the LORD spoke to Abram in a vision and said to him, "Do not be afraid, Abram, for I will protect you, and your reward will be great." (Genesis 15:1).

The Lord will protect me, and my household, and reward us greatly. We will not be afraid.

And Moses said unto the people, Fear ye not, stand still, and see the salvation of the Lord , which he will shew to you to day:

for the Egyptians whom ye have seen to day, ye shall see them again no more for ever (Exodus 14:13 KJV).

The Lord will sink all my adversaries, I will not fear; I await the salvation of the Lord, in Jesus' name. Amen!

Ye shall not fear them: for the Lord your God he shall fight for you (Deuteronomy 3:22 KJV).

My God will fight for me. I will not fear any opposition.

I, who dwell in the secret place of the Most High Shall abide under the shadow of the Almighty. I will say of the Lord, "He is my refuge and my fortress; My God, in Him I will trust." Surely He shall deliver me from the snare of the fowler and from the perilous pestilence. He shall cover me with His feathers, and under His wings I shall take refuge; His truth shall be my shield and buckler. I shall not be afraid of the terror by night, nor of the arrow that flies by day, Nor of the pestilence that walks in darkness, Nor of the destruction that lays waste at noonday. A thousand may fall at my side, and ten thousand at my right hand; but it shall not come near me. Only with my eyes shall I look, and see the reward of the wicked. Because I have made the Lord , who is my refuge, even the Most High, my dwelling place, no evil shall befall me, nor shall any plague come near my dwelling; For He shall give His angels charge over me, to keep me in all my ways. In their hands they shall bear me up, lest I dash my foot against a stone. I shall tread upon the lion and the cobra, the young lion and the serpent I shall trample underfoot. "Because I have set my love upon Him, therefore He will deliver me; He will set me on high, because I have known His name. I shall call upon Him, and He will answer me; He will be with me in trouble; He will deliver me and honor me.

With long life He will satisfy me, and show me His salvation," in Jesus' name. Amen! (Psalm 91: 1-16 NKJV) personalized.

I will lift up mine eyes unto the hills, from whence cometh my help. [2] My help cometh from the Lord, which made heaven and earth. [3] He will not suffer my foot to be moved: he that keepeth me will not slumber. [4] Behold, he that keepeth Israel shall neither slumber nor sleep. [5] The Lord is my keeper: the Lord is my shade upon my right hand. [6] The sun shall not smite me by day, nor the moon by night. [7] The Lord shall preserve me from all evil: he shall preserve my soul. [8] The Lord shall preserve my going out and my coming in from this time forth, and even for evermore, in Jesus' name. Amen! (Psalm 121: 1-8 KJV) personalized.

Woman of Virtue

Favour is deceitful, and beauty is vain: but a woman that feareth the Lord, she shall be praised (Proverbs 31:30 KJV).

I decree the fear of the Lord over my life, in Jesus' name. Amen!

When she speaks, her words are wise, and she gives instructions with kindness (Proverbs 31:26 KJV).

The words that come out of me will be words of wisdom, given with kindness, in Jesus' name. Amen!

She extends a helping hand to the poor and opens her arms to the needy (Proverbs 31:20).

My arms are open to the poor and needy, giving helping hand as much as I can, in Jesus' name. Amen!

The heart of her husband doth safely trust in her, so that he shall have no need of spoil (Proverbs 31:11 KJV).

The heart of my husband will safely trust me; I will greatly enrich his life all the days of my life, in Jesus' name. Amen!

A worthy wife is a crown for her husband, but a disgraceful woman is like cancer in his bones (Proverbs 12:4).
I decree that I'm a crown for my husband, and not cancer in his bones, in Jesus' name. Amen!

It's better to live alone in the corner of an attic than with a quarrelsome wife in a lovely home. It's better to live alone in the desert than with a quarrelsome, complaining wife (Proverbs 21:9, 19).
I forbid every complaining or quarrelsome spirit in me, in Jesus' name. Amen!

Fathers can give their sons an inheritance of houses and wealth, but only the LORD can give an understanding wife (Proverbs 19:14).
I choose to be an understanding wife. Make me one Lord, in Jesus' name. Amen!

For women who claim to be devoted to God should make themselves attractive by the good things they do (1 Timothy 2:10).
My good works makes me attractive. Help me to do more Lord, in Jesus' name. Amen!

You should clothe yourselves instead with the beauty that comes from within, the unfading beauty of a gentle and quiet spirit, which is so precious to God (1 Peter 3:4).

I clothe myself with the beauty that comes from within: the unfading beauty of a gentle and quiet spirit, which is so precious to God.

This is how the holy women of old made themselves beautiful. They put their trust in God and accepted the authority of their husbands (1 Peter 3:5).

I put my trust in God and accept the authority of my husband, in Jesus' name. Amen!

A wise woman builds her home, but a foolish woman tears it down with her own hands (Proverbs 14:1).

The wisdom of God in me will help me build and not tear down, in Jesus' name. Amen!

A house is built by wisdom and becomes strong through good sense. [4] Through knowledge its rooms are filled with all sorts of precious riches and valuables (Proverbs 24:3-4).

I receive the wisdom, knowledge and understanding to build a strong family, in Jesus' name. Amen!

The Real Man

I will sing of your love and justice, LORD. I will praise you with songs. [2] I will be careful to live a blameless life—when will you come to help me? I will lead a life of integrity in my own home. [3] I will refuse to look at anything vile and vulgar. I hate all who deal crookedly; I will have nothing to do with them. [4] I will reject perverse ideas and stay away from every evil. [5] I will not tolerate people who slander their neighbors. I will not endure conceit and pride. [6] I will search for faithful people to be my companions. Only those who are above reproach will be allowed to serve me. [7] I will not allow deceivers to serve in my house, and liars will not stay in my presence. [8] My daily task will be to ferret out the wicked and free the city of the LORD from their grip (Psalm 101:1-8) Personalized.

I made a covenant with my eyes not to look with lust at a young woman (Job 31:1).

The Real Man

I will drink water from my own well–share my love only with my wife. [16] I will not spill the water of my springs in the streets, having sex with just anyone? [17] I will reserve it for ourselves. Will never share it with strangers. [18] I will let my wife be a fountain of blessing for me. I will rejoice in the wife of my youth. [19] She is a loving deer, a graceful doe. I let her breasts satisfy me always. I will always be captivated by her love. [20] I will not be captivated, by an immoral woman, or fondle the breasts of a promiscuous woman [21] For the LORD sees clearly what a man does, examining every path he takes. [22] I will not be held captive by my own sins; they are ropes that catch and hold him. [23] I will not die for lack of self-control; I will not be lost because of my great foolishness (Proverbs 5:15-23) Personalized.

It is not for kings, O Lemuel, it is not for kings to drink wine; nor for princes strong drink: [5] Lest they drink, and forget the law, and pervert the judgment of any of the afflicted. [6] Give strong drink unto him that is ready to perish, and wine unto those that be of heavy hearts (Proverbs 31:4-6 KJV).

Strong drink is for those ready to perish. It's not for me to drink neither wine nor strong drink: lest I drink and forget the law of God, and have weak judgment.

Looking unto Jesus the author and finisher of our faith; who for the joy that was set before him endured the cross, despising the shame, and is set down at the right hand of the throne of God (Hebrews 12:2 KJV)

I choose to fix my eyes on Jesus the author and finisher of my faith.

Mercy

It is of the Lord's mercies that we are not consumed, because his compassions fail not. [23] They are new every morning: great is thy faithfulness (Lamentations 3:22-23 KJV).

The faithfulness of the Lord is great. I thank You Lord for new mercies every day of my life.

Behold now, thy servant hath found grace in thy sight, and thou hast magnified thy mercy, which thou hast shewed unto me in saving my life; and I cannot escape to the mountain, lest some evil take me, and I die: (Genesis 19:19 KJV).

I thank You Lord, for Your mercy that is magnified in my life.

But my mercy shall not depart away from him, as I took it from Saul, whom I put away before thee (2 Samuel 7:15 KJV).

I decree that the Lord's mercy will not depart from: me, my household, and my church, in Jesus' name. Amen!

Mercy

But the Lord was with Joseph, and shewed him mercy, and gave him favour in the sight of the keeper of the prison (Genesis 39:21 KJV).

Joseph found favor in a strange land. I decree the favor of God will locate me wherever I dwell, in Jesus' name. Amen!

Surely goodness and mercy shall follow me all the days of my life: and I will dwell in the house of the Lord for ever (Psalm 23:6 KJV).

I decree that the goodness and mercy of the Lord shall follow me all of my days and I will dwell in God's house forever, in Jesus' name. Amen!

Many sorrows shall be to the wicked: but he that trusteth in the Lord, mercy shall compass him about (Psalm 32:10 KJV).

The mercy of the Lord compasses me and my household, round about because we trust in Him.

I cried out, "I am slipping!" but your unfailing love, O LORD, supported me (Psalm 94:18).

Thank You Jesus for your unfailing love that holds me on; I cannot slip away, in Jesus' name. Amen!

Behold, as the eyes of servants look unto the hand of their masters, and as the eyes of a maiden unto the hand of her mistress; so our eyes wait upon the Lord our God, until that he have mercy upon us (Psalm 123:2 KJV).

My eyes are upon you oh Lord; I know you will have mercy on me, in Jesus' name. Amen!

The Lord will perfect that which concerneth me: thy mercy, O Lord, endureth for ever: forsake not the works of thine own hands (Psalm 138:8 KJV).
The Lord will perfect all that concern me, and every member of my family; we will not be forsaken, in Jesus' name. Amen!

He that covereth his sins shall not prosper: but whoso confesseth and forsaketh them shall have mercy (Proverbs 28:13 KJV).
Almighty God, I confess my sins.......according to your word; please have mercy on me, in Jesus' name. Amen!

I have observed something else under the sun. The fastest runner doesn't always win the race, and the strongest warrior doesn't always win the battle. The wise sometimes go hungry, and the skillful are not necessarily wealthy. And those who are educated don't always lead successful lives. It is all decided by chance, by being in the right place at the right time (Ecclesiastes 9:11).
Lord, by your mercy let me always be at the right place at the right time, in Jesus' name. Amen!

Church Growth

F ear not: for I am with thee: I will bring thy seed from the east, and gather thee from the west;
I will say to the north, Give up; and to the south, Keep not back: bring my sons from far, and my daughters from the ends of the earth; (Isaiah 43:5-6 KJV).

The Lord will gather all that are ordained to be members of.....from all corners of the earth. They will not rest until they locate......, in Jesus' name. Amen!

You will arise and have mercy on Jerusalem- and now is the time to pity her, now is the time you promised to help (Psalm 102:13).

The mercy of God, will prevail in every project in my family and Church family; God will make provision available, in Jesus' name. Amen!

And out of them shall proceed thanksgiving and the voice of them that make merry: and I will multiply them, and they shall not be few; I will also glorify them, and they shall not be small (Jeremiah 30:19 KJV).

The Lord will increase, multiply and glorify His Church.......; thanksgiving and rejoicing will not cease in our midst, in Jesus' name. Amen!

A little one shall become a thousand, and a small one a strong nation: I the Lord will hasten it in his time (Isaiah 60:22 KJV).

God of multiplication, You will bring it to pass; Your word will not fall to the ground. Your Church..... will grow into a strong nation, in Jesus' name. Amen!

Though thy beginning was small, yet thy latter end should greatly increase (Job 8:7 KJV).

The increase of Your Church......... is inevitable; its latter end shall greatly increase in accordance to your word, in Jesus' name. Amen!

And I say also unto thee, That thou art Peter, and upon this rock I will build my church; and the gates of hell shall not prevail against it (Matthew 16:18 KJV).

Lord, you're the builder of your Church........; no gate of hell can prevail against it, in Jesus' name. Amen!

Yes, think about Abraham, your ancestor, and Sarah, who gave birth to your nation. Abraham was only one man when I called him. But when I blessed him, he became a great nation." (Isaiah 51:2)

The blessing of the Lord makes great. Your blessing is upon Your Church..........; It shall be great, in Jesus' name. Amen!

People from many nations will come and say, "Come, let us go up to the mountain of the LORD, to the house of Jacob's God. There he will teach us his ways, and we will walk in his paths." For the LORD's teaching will go out from Zion; his word will go out from Jerusalem (Micah 4:2).

The gate of your church ...... is open to people from all Nations. You will draw them in, from all directions, in Jesus' name. Amen!

Even though the destroyer has destroyed Judah, the LORD will restore its honor. Israel's vine has been stripped of branches, but he will restore its splendor (Nahum 2:2).

Lord we trust You will restore the honor of your Church........ in Jesus name. Amen!

Seeing it is a righteous thing with God to recompense tribulation to them that trouble you; (2 Thessalonians 1:6 KJV).

Lord according to Your word every one who persecute your Church, will be persecuted. Persecute everyone that rise against your Church........, in Jesus' name. Amen!

Therefore said he unto them, The harvest truly is great, but the labourers are few: pray ye therefore the Lord of the harvest, that he would send forth labourers into his harvest (Luke 10:2 KJV).

Lord of Harvest, we trust You to send laborers into Your Church.........; co laborers that will help populate Your kingdom and increase Your vineyard, in Jesus' name. Amen!

And a certain woman named Lydia, a seller of purple, of the city of Thyatira, which worshipped God, heard us : whose heart the Lord opened, that she attended unto the things which were spoken of Paul (Acts 16:14 KJV).

Lord, the same way You opened the heart of Lydia, You'll open the heart of all we reach out to with the gospel of our Lord Jesus Christ, in Jesus' name. Amen!

Children

For I know him, that he will command his children and his household after him, and they shall keep the way of the Lord , to do justice and judgment; that the Lord may bring upon Abraham that which he hath spoken of him (Genesis 18:19 KJV).

I decree that my children will keep the way of the Lord, they will do what is right and just; they will live a life that please God, in Jesus' name. Amen!

The Lord shall increase you more and more, you and your children (Psalm 115:14 KJV).

I declare increase over my life, and the lives of my Children–generations after me, in Jesus' name. Amen!

Children are a gift from the LORD; they are a reward from him (Psalm 127:3).

My Children are a gift and reward from the Lord; I receive the grace to nurture them in the way of the Lord.

Your wife will be like a fruitful grapevine, flourishing within your home. Your children will be like vigorous young olive trees as they sit around your table (Psalm 128:3).

I declare strength and vigor over my Children; none of them will be a weakling, in Jesus' name. Amen!

And all thy children shall be taught of the Lord; and great shall be the peace of thy children (Isaiah 54:13 KJV).

I decree that my children will be doers of the word, they will dwell in the truth and live by it; great shall be their peace, in Jesus name. Amen!

In those days they shall say no more, The fathers have eaten a sour grape, and the children's teeth are set on edge (Jeremiah 31:29 KJV).

I decree that the teeth of my children will not be set on edge over my iniquity; they will not suffer as a result of my mistakes, in Jesus' name. Amen!

But thus saith the Lord , Even the captives of the mighty shall be taken away, and the prey of the terrible shall be delivered: for I will contend with him that contendeth with thee, and I will save thy children (Isaiah 49:25 KJV).

Thank You Lord for contending with any force that contend with me and my children; You will save us from the numerous attacks of the enemy, in Jesus' name. Amen!

Praise the LORD! How joyful are those who fear the LORD and delight in obeying his commands. [2] Their children will be successful everywhere; an entire generation of godly people will be blessed (Psalm 112:1-2).

My children and their children will be great in my lifetime in Jesus' name. Amen!

And I will pour out my Spirit on your descendants, and my blessing on your children. They will thrive like watered grass, like willows on a riverbank (Isaiah 44: 3b, 4).

I thank You Lord, for pouring Your Spirit upon my seed; the Spirit of excellence, the Spirit of greatness. My Children shall be great leaders of their generation. They remain blessed, in Jesus' name. Amen!

They shall not build, and another inhabit; they shall not plant, and another eat: for as the days of a tree are the days of my people, and mine elect shall long enjoy the work of their hands (Isaiah 65:22 KJV).

I decree that my labor over my children will not be in vain; I will live long enough to enjoy the fruit of my hard work. I shall not labor in vain, in Jesus' name. Amen!

My child, fear the LORD and the king. Don't associate with rebels, [22] for disaster will hit them suddenly. Who knows what punishment will come from the LORD and the king? (Proverbs 24:21-22).

My children will not be found with the rebellious but with the saints of God, in Jesus' name. Amen!

Teenagers

Don't let the excitement of youth cause you to forget your Creator. Honor him in your youth before you grow old and say, "Life is not pleasant anymore." (Ecclesiastes 12: 1).

I choose to honor God in my youth, with my strength, and everything within me. I receive all the grace I need, in Jesus' name. Amen!

Let us hear the conclusion of the whole matter: Fear God, and keep his commandments: for this is the whole duty of man (Ecclesiastes 12: 13 KJV).

I decree that the fear of God will rule my heart, unto obeying the word of God, in Jesus' name. Amen!

He renews my strength. He guides me along right paths, bringing honor to his name (Psalm 23: 3).

I thank You Lord for renewing my strength, and guiding me along right paths, in Jesus' name. Amen!

He gives power to the weak and strength to the powerless (Isaiah 40: 29).

I receive strength and divine ability, to excel in all I lay my hands on, in Jesus' name. Amen!

So I say, let the Holy Spirit guide your lives. Then you won't be doing what your sinful nature craves (Galatians 5: 16).

I submit to you Holy Spirit to guide me, in my everyday choices, in Jesus' name

For God is working in you, giving you the desire and the power to do what pleases Him (Philippians 2: 13).

The Lord is at work in me putting in me a strong desire to please Him, in Jesus' name. Amen!

so that no one can criticize you. Live clean, innocent lives as children of God, shining like bright lights in a world full of crooked and perverse people (Philippians 2: 15).

I choose to live clean, innocent life; shining like bright lights in this dark world, in Jesus' name. Amen!

All the others care only for themselves and not for what matters to Jesus Christ (Philippians 2: 21).

I choose to care for the things that matter to my savior, in Jesus' name. Amen!

Yet now he has reconciled you to himself through the death of Christ in his physical body. As a result, he has brought you into his own presence, and you are holy and blameless as you stand before him without a single fault (Colossians 1:22).

I'm reconciled to God. I now stand before Him Holy and blameless without a single fault, in Jesus' name. Amen!

And now, just as you accepted Christ Jesus as your Lord, you must continue to follow him. [7] Let your roots grow down into him, and let your lives be built on him. Then your faith will grow strong in the truth you were taught, and you will overflow with thankfulness (Colossians 2:6-7).

I decree that: I will continue in You, my roots will grow down into You, my life will be built on You and my faith will grow strong in you day by day, in Jesus' name. Amen!

When you came to Christ, you were "circumcised," but not by a physical procedure. Christ performed a spiritual circumcision–the cutting away of your sinful nature (Colossians 2: 11).

I decree that my sinful nature has been cut off, when I came to Christ; I now live a life of purity, in Jesus' name. Amen!

For you died to this life, and your real life is hidden with Christ in God. And when Christ, who is your life, is revealed to the whole world, you will share in all his glory. So put to death the sinful, earthly things lurking within you. Have nothing to do with sexual immorality, impurity, lust, and evil desires (Colossians 3: 3, 4).

Teenagers

I choose not to have anything to do with: sexual immorality, impurity, lust, and evil desires. I choose to live a clean life in Jesus' name. Amen!

He guards the paths of the just and protects those who are faithful to him. [9] Then you will understand what is right, just, and fair, and you will find the right way to go (Proverbs 2:8-9).

I receive direction from the Lord, that I may understand what is: right, just, fair and the right way to go, in Jesus' name. Amen!

[10] For wisdom will enter your heart, and knowledge will fill you with joy. [11] Wise choices will watch over you. Understanding will keep you safe (Proverbs 2: 10, 11).

I receive God's wisdom, knowledge and understanding, that I may make wise choices in life. Help me Lord.

Wisdom will save you from the immoral woman, from the seductive words of the promiscuous woman (Proverbs 2: 16).

The Holy Spirit will guide me far away from the immoral and promiscuous woman, in Jesus' name. Amen!

Follow the steps of good men instead, and stay on the paths of the righteous (Proverbs 2:20).

I will stay along the path of the righteous all the days of my life, in Jesus' name. Amen!

But you must remain faithful to the things you have been taught. You know they are true, for you know you can trust those who taught you (2 Timothy 3: 14).

I will remain faithful to all I've been taught, in Jesus' name. Amen!

For the angel of the LORD is a guard; he surrounds and defends all who fear him (Psalm 34:7).

Thank you Lord for protecting me and my family at all times.

May God give you more and more grace and peace as you grow in your knowledge of God and Jesus our Lord (2 Peter 1:2).

I receive more and more grace, and peace even as I grow in the knowledge of the Lord, in Jesus' name. Amen.

Don't be afraid, for I am with you. Don't be discouraged, for I am your God. I will strengthen you and help you. I will hold you up with my victorious right hand (Isaiah 41:10).

The Lord will keep and preserve me; he will hold me up with His victorious right hand in Jesus' name. Amen!

The thief cometh not, but for to steal, and to kill, and to destroy: I am come that they might have life, and that they might have it more abundantly (John 10: 10 KJV).

I thank you Lord for abundant life in Christ Jesus.

For ye were sometimes darkness, but now are ye light in the Lord: walk as children of light: (Ephesians 5: 8 KJV).

I receive the grace to walk in the path of light; no act of darkness will be found in me, in Jesus' name. Amen!

For the authorities do not strike fear in people who are doing right, but in those who are doing wrong. Would you like to live without fear of the authorities? Do what is right, and they will honor you (Romans 13:3).

I will live without fear of the authorities, always doing what is right at all times, in Jesus' name. Amen!

Like newborn babies, you must crave pure spiritual milk so that you will grow into a full experience of salvation. Cry out for this nourishment, (1 Peter 2:2).

I receive a sincere hunger of God's word in my heart, that I may grow into a full experience of salvation, in Jesus' name. Amen.

We know that God's children do not make a practice of sinning, for God's Son holds them securely, and the evil one cannot touch them (1 John 5:18).

I receive the grace to keep myself pure, in Jesus' name. Amen!

But Daniel was determined not to defile himself by eating the food and wine given to them by the king. He asked the chief of staff for permission not to eat these unacceptable foods (Daniel 1: 8).

I choose not to defile myself in any way, in Jesus' name. Amen!

The way of a fool is right in his own eyes: but he that hearkeneth unto counsel is wise (Proverbs 12:15 KJV).
I choose to listen to counsel. I will not go the way of a fool, in Jesus' name. Amen!

Don't you realize that your body is the temple of the Holy Spirit, who lives in you and was given to you by God? You do not belong to yourself, (1 Corinthians 6:19).
My body is the temple of the Holy Spirit; I will keep it pure in Jesus' name. Amen!

If we confess our sins, he is faithful and just to forgive us our sins, and to cleanse us from all unrighteousness (1John 1:9).
I confess my sins......; cleanse me Lord from all unrighteousness, in Jesus' name. Amen!

Dear friends, I warn you as "temporary residents and foreigners" to keep away from worldly desires that wage war against your very souls (1 Peter 2:11).
I choose to stay away from every worldly desire, so I can preserve my soul.

My child, fear the LORD and the king. Don't associate with rebels, [22] for disaster will hit them suddenly. Who knows what punishment will come from the LORD and the king? (Proverbs 24:21-22).

I will not be found with the rebellious but with the saints of God, in Jesus' name. Amen!

As for these four children, God gave them knowledge and skill in all learning and wisdom: and Daniel had understanding in all visions and dreams (Daniel 1:17 KJV).

I receive knowledge and skill in all learning and wisdom, in Jesus' name. Amen!

Daniel soon proved himself more capable than all the other administrators and high officers. Because of Daniel's great ability, the king made plans to place him over the entire empire (Daniel 6:3).

I decree the same excellent Spirit found in Daniel is in me, it will single me out for strange blessings and promotions, in Jesus' name. Amen!

About the Author

Funmi Uzoma – A dynamic woman of faith, has a way of igniting people she come in contact with, with the power of God. She gave her life to Christ in 1985 in Lagos, Nigeria and since then has been serving the Lord fervently. She believes God has the final verdict on any issue of life. She has been in ministry since 1995 serving faithfully alongside her husband. She is a Graduate of Accounting and an Ordained Minister of God in The Redeemed Christian Church of God. She is a highly skillful and talented woman, full of vision. She is married to Joel Uzoma and has been a tremendous support to him in Ministry from the day of his call. Together they pastor a parish of the Redeemed Christian Church of God 'Dayspring Chapel' in Houston Texas, USA. Their marriage is blessed with a wonderful son.

www.ingramcontent.com/pod-product-compliance
Ingram Content Group UK Ltd.
Pitfield, Milton Keynes, MK11 3LW, UK
UKHW022216230426
12048UKWH00016BA/870